Coming to England

FLOELLA BENJAMIN

An Inspiring True Story Celebrating the Windrush Generation

Coming to England

The true story of
Dame Floella Benjamin

Illustrated by
JOELLE AVELINO

MACMILLAN CHILDREN'S BOOKS

First published 2016 by Macmillan Children's Books

This edition published 2021 by Macmillan Children's Books
an imprint of Pan Macmillan
The Smithson, 6 Briset Street, London EC1M 5NR
EU representative: Macmillan Publishers Ireland Ltd, 1st Floor,
The Liffey Trust Centre, 117–126 Sheriff Street Upper,
Dublin 1, D01 YC43
Associated companies throughout the world
www.panmacmillan.com

ISBN 978-1-5290-4544-4

9

A CIP catalogue record for this book is available from the British Library.

Printed and bound by CPI Group (UK) Ltd, Croydon CR0 4YY

This book is dedicated to Marmie, Dardie, Sandra,
Lester, Ellington, Roy Jnr and Cynthia

Contents

Foreword

I always say that childhood lasts a lifetime, so I wrote this book twenty-six years ago through the eyes of a child to give people, both black and white, an insight into the circumstances that brought a whole generation of West Indians to Britain and the struggles they experienced. I tried, through my own journey, to share what many of them had to go through in order to make the difficult and sometimes painful transition to a new life in the fabled motherland, the 'Land of Hope and Glory'.

Since the book's first publication, many amazing things have happened to me and so many public appointments have come my way, including becoming a Baroness in the House of Lords in 2010 and becoming a Dame in 2020 for my charitable contribution to British society. I often wonder who would have thought this possible, considering what I had to endure when I first arrived in England in 1960.

In the late 1950s and early 1960s, hundreds of

West Indians left their glorious Caribbean islands to come to Great Britain. For these pioneers it was a time of excitement and discovery. It was like falling into the arms of someone you had been brought up to love. The pioneers brought with them their music, joy, colour, style and culture and they were quite prepared to share these wonders. But for many the experience turned out to be quite opposite to the expectation. They soon began to feel inferior and were rarely allowed to take pride in the various talents they had to offer in the rebuilding of Great Britain after the war.

For their children who had been left at home it was not a happy time. They had no choice when the decision to leave was made. The grief started when they were removed from the bosom of happy family life, many not realising that their parents were going away.

Some children were left 'overnight' with relatives or friends only to wake up to a lonely, cruel existence of great hardship with the very people entrusted to look after them while their parents set up home in Britain. When they were finally sent for to join their parents they expected the reunion to bring joy and happiness, yet they were to experience only rejection and worse once they arrived.

To feel you belong is a most important necessity in life. This feeling was denied to thousands of West Indian children who came to Britain, but at least they had their fond memories of the homes they left, where they were recognised a person, not a colour. The next generation however, who were born into an adopted country, would not know enough about their roots and how they came to be living in Britain. Today my story also reflects the experiences of children from many other countries around the world who have arrived on these shores for various reasons. They too have felt rejection and have had to face adversity.

I know that if they are given opportunities in the way I eventually was, they too can work towards making Britain their true home and a country of which they will be proud. My mum always told me and my five siblings that education would be our passport to a better life; that our achievements would contribute to a better world and make a difference. We have all been successful in our chosen careers and I strongly believe that our own children will use their education to the same effect. It has been rewarding for me to know that telling my story in *Coming to England* has, in some small way, helped people to find their identity, to discover their history and where they came from and to feel proud of themselves.

Baroness Floella Benjamin, DBE DL

Chapter One
Life in Trinidad

The day my brother Ellington was born, my elder sister Sandra, who was four, my brother Lester, who was two, and I, aged three, were all out on the gallery – that's what we called the veranda. My mother, whom we affectionately named Marmie, had told us that if we looked hard enough we would see a stork flying high in the sky with our new baby. I was hungry and

really wanted Marmie to make one of her delicious soups for us, but I dared not take my eyes off the sky just in case I missed the big arrival.

Anyway, Mrs Jackson, the local midwife who lived in the lane opposite our house, said we couldn't come into the house to see my mother until she called us.

I was beginning to feel more and more hungry, tired and anxious but I still kept my eyes glued to the heavens. Suddenly I heard the loud cry of a newborn baby. I felt happy but disappointed at the same time because I hadn't seen the stork arrive. My mother told us it had come through the back door. I looked for it years later when my brother Roy and sister Cynthia arrived. Mrs Jackson was always there but I never spotted that elusive stork coming through the front or the back door!

The house we lived in was a small wooden building on stilts with dazzling whitewashed walls. There were windows and doors at the front and the back. We had two bedrooms which were the scene of many pillow fights and trampolining sessions, a small washroom, with a sink and cold tap, an airy kitchen with a large glassless louvred window where we also ate all our meals, and finally a sitting room where no one was allowed except on special occasions or when we had visitors.

This room was my mother's pride and joy. Its brilliant white curtains always smelt fresh and the mahogany furniture was always highly polished, as was the wooden floor. My sister and I spent many hours polishing and shining that room from as far back as I can remember. We had to do the polishing before we left for school each day. The comfortable wooden chairs in the room were draped with crisp white lace headrests and the round table, which we ate from on Sundays and other special occasions, had a doily in its centre, on which sat a vase of glorious fresh flowers. These were from our small front garden, which was full of exotic, sweet-smelling flowers and shrubs such as beautiful flame-red hibiscus which seemed to attract swarms of exquisite butterflies and hovering humming birds, in search of nectar. The back yard was where Marmie grew vegetables for our kitchen, like pigeon peas, cassavas, okras and dasheen. A tall bushy tree stood in the yard, reaching

up to the kitchen window, and whenever one of us had a bad cold Marmie would pick some of the leaves, boil them and give us the vile-tasting liquid to drink. It always made us better – I guess the thought of a second dose was enough to do the trick! Also in the yard was a galvanized shower unit where we had our baths. There was no hot tap but the cold water was always warm because of the heat of the sun. During the drought season, from around July to September, we would have to get water from a standpipe in the street. Everyone would queue up with large enamel buckets, oil cans, basins – anything big enough to carry the water. The washing was done under the house in a big wooden tub with a scrubbing board, and the washing lines hung between two trees in the back yard. Our car was also parked under the house.

At the very bottom of the yard was the latrine, the outside toilet. It was a small wooden hut and none of the planks of wood quite met, allowing chinks of light to shine through.

Inside was a four-metre deep hole, reinforced with concrete. A wooden seat was built on top like a throne. The lock for the door was a piece of string which was hooked over a large nail. The square pieces of toilet paper, cut out of sheets of newspaper, hung on one of the walls. The comic strip pages always made good reading, but the only problem was you could never finish a story because the last part had inevitably been chopped off to make another sheet.

I didn't mind using the latrine during the day. I would imagine myself as a queen sitting on a throne holding court. But in the evening it was a different story. The scratching sound of the crickets, the loud deep croaks of the toads, the buzzing and flashing sparks of the night insects was enough to drive any child's imagination wild and I was no exception.

I hated having to visit that dark hole – even the flickering light of my candle was no defence or comfort.

I liked sitting on the gallery after dark, though. We would sit there at night on the two rocking chairs with my father, Dardie, who used to tell us some amazing tales: his own stories as well as Anancy stories, the tales that came from Africa to the Carribbean. Dardie was born in Antigua and came to Trinidad, where he met Marmie, when he was nineteen. So he would tell us about his homeland, and about the capitals of the world – where they were and how many people lived there. We were quizzed on these night after night. He also gave us vivid descriptions of American movies and filmstars and we were each given a filmstar's name as well as a pet name. Mine was Martha Raye because I used to love to dance and sing like her. In fact we each had to do a party piece before we went to bed, parading and performing up and down the gallery like superstars. There was no television so we had to make our own entertainment. But once a month he would take us to see a film at the cinema in San Fernando.

Dardie felt it was his duty to open our eyes and minds to the world even though we lived on a small island just a few miles from South America. He always found time to play with us even though he worked hard as a field policeman. He patrolled the huge oil refinery at Point-a-Pierre which was near the oil field Forest Reserves in the southwest of the island. He wore a khaki uniform with brass buttons which we all took great pride in polishing every night so they would glitter in the sunshine like gold. We always ran to meet him on his way from work and he would carry us home like a strong giant, two under his arms and two on his shoulders, while the two youngest watched. Then he would toss us in the air like acrobats. Oh what excitement! We didn't always have our meals with Dardie because he worked shifts, but we would crowd around him whenever he had his meals.

Food played a very important part in our lives. Marmie insisted that we had plenty of it and her cupboards were never empty. She insisted we all ate well so that we would grow up big and strong. Mind you we didn't need much encouragement – it was always a race to see who finished first or ate the most food. Not a scrap was ever left on the plates.

For breakfast we would have fresh home-baked bread, scrambled eggs or saltfish, fresh fruits and tea, which could mean anything from fresh grated cocoa, coffee or tea itself. After breakfast we had to line up to be given a dose of cod liver oil which was hideous.

The fishy, oily liquid seemed to line the inside of the throat and stay there. It was one of the few things I didn't want to be first in line for and when it was my turn I used to hold my nose and only the promise of a piece of orange would encourage me to take it. Marmie told us it was good for our bones and teeth, which was true but it didn't make it taste any better.

For lunch it was either a rich tasty soup which was like a stew made of meat, pulses, vegetables and dumplings, or rice served with beef, chicken or, on Fridays, fish. For dessert we had whatever fresh fruit was in season: mangoes, pineapples, pawpaw or pomsitea, and for supper we had bread and cakes, all baked by Marmie, washed down with cocoa.

Saturday was Marmie's baking day, and she would bake enough for the whole week. Bread or bakes – a sort of bread with no yeast, sweet bread – bread with coconut and sugar, sponge cakes and coconut drops. The smell of her freshly baked bread and cakes was wonderful – it always made me hungry. Sandra and I had to do our bit by helping to grease the baking tins and stir the cake mixture. The best part was when we fought over licking the cake bowl.

Sunday was a special day in Trinidad. It was the one time of the week when we all got together, which gave me a happy feeling of belonging and a sense of occasion. The realization that the family unit was special began to take place during that time. We ate lavishly in the sitting room: the crisp, starched, white tablecloth would be spread out over the mahogany table, and the best glasses – frosted coloured ones – and plates were used. Then the table would be laden with dishes of food – it was like a feast. On the menu was brown down chicken, rice, plantains, callaloo, sweet potatoes, cassavas, gungo peas, macaroni cheese pie. To drink we would have soursop juice or limeade made from the fresh fruit and ice bought by my mother from the ice truck which came round every day. Not many people had refrigerators so the big blocks of ice would be wrapped in sackcloth and newspaper and would be kept in a big wooden tub. Pieces of ice would be broken off with an ice pick which was very sharp.

For dessert Dardie would make ice cream in a special ice cream tub. It was a thick metal churn inside a wooden tub with ice, salt and newspaper crammed between the two. The ice cream mixture was made up of custard powder, fresh vanilla, condensed milk, sugar and gelatine. He would always drop five cents into the churn and when the ice cream was served the lucky person who found the coin would keep it. We all excitedly took turns to churn the container round and round to make the ice cream set which seemed to take forever.

When Marmie was not cooking she was doing other household chores, and while she worked she sang songs. She didn't have a particularly good voice but that didn't stop her. Her singing was very infectious, so whenever we helped her we sang too. She sang whilst she washed, cooked, cleaned and ironed. The iron she used was a big heavy cast-iron one with hot coals inside it. She had to wrap a towel around the handle to hold it because it was so hot. Marmie also made all our clothes, even down to our knickers and petticoats. Most people made their own clothes but Marmie was always creative in what she made for us to wear. She had style, a real flair for fashion. People often used to stop and admire all six of us when we were dressed and out with her and Dardie.

The job Marmie seemed to love doing best was shopping at the local market. What a spectacular event that was. The market was a big concrete two-storey building with steps leading up to it. There were concrete slabs where the stallholders displayed their wares. Meat, fruit and vegetables had to be bought fresh every day. The smell was intoxicating: the air was full of the scent of fruit and spices mixed with a tinge of sea and sun. At the busy, bustling market the noise was deafening. The stallholders tried to

outshout each other as they attempted to attract the
attention of the customers. The customers, in turn,
haggled over prices. You could buy anything there:
live chickens, breadfruit, sugar cane, cocoa pods,
pineapples, rice, sweet potatoes, sweetcorn, guavas,
yams, dasheen, limes, grapefruit, mangoes, tomatoes,
cassava and enormous watermelons. Watermelons
have a special association for me because of the day
I saw some unceremoniously topple out of a truck.
It was on one of the many days when Marmie had
sent Sandra and I to the market with a shopping

list, some dollars and cents and instructions not to overspend but to get the best things. On the way to the market we saw a stray dog run across the road in front of a truck full of juicy watermelons. The driver had to slam on his brakes so hard that the flimsy wooden sides of the truck collapsed, sending the ripe watermelons cascading on to the road and leaving it awash in a sea of red mush. Shoppers scattered as the melons tumbled down the street – they, like us, could not stop themselves from laughing but the driver was furious. The dog disappeared into the crowd but the red colour of the watermelons stained the road for days.

It was also a great adventure whenever we had to buy fish. Sandra and I used to hold hands and skip down the lane to the wharf where the fishermen sold their catch. Fish of all sizes were on sale: red snappers, herrings, butterfish, barracudas, crabs, shrimps and lobsters. Once we were privileged to witness a fisherman's dream – the biggest fish imaginable. It was about three times the size of me. The fisherman, who was the star of the day, had caught a shark and as customers gathered round to touch and admire the

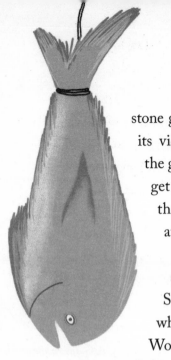

stone grey giant of a fish as it hung high, its vicious grinning mouth pointing to the ground, I pushed my way forward to get a closer look. I came eye to eye with the huge monster, and as I stared back at it I was convinced it winked at me.

Marmie sometimes took us shopping in the big towns, like San Fernando and Port of Spain, where there were large stores like Woolworths. There were also furniture stores as well as stores selling fabrics, books and shoes. These were very similar to the stores in any big city. I really didn't like going to them because Marmie would always tell us not to touch the glass counters in case we broke them. I much preferred going to Mr Ching's shop, which was like an Aladdin's cave. It was our local corner shop and sold everything from scrubbing brushes and soap to butter and powdered milk, from shoelaces and matches to sweets and candles.

I found joy and pleasure in the simplest things. It took very little to make me happy because Marmie had taught us all how to be contented with what we had, how to make our lot seem the best in the world. I had learned from an early age how to have pride in myself and my country. During this period of my life everything seemed perfect.

Chapter Two
School Life

The first school I ever went to was not far from my house. I was four years old at the time and every morning Sandra and I would walk there, dressed in our white blouses and blue tunics, our hair plaited immaculately. Marmie used to inspect us before we left because the teachers were very strict about school uniform – and everything else, come to think of it. Each morning there would be an inspection by the headmistress to make sure our nails, clothes and shoes were clean. We would have to line up in the school yard. The latecomers would try to sneak on to the end of the lines but the headmistress seemed to have eyes in the back of her head and would always spot them. I was late once and I thought I would catch her out. I willed myself to be invisible. I felt sure I could sneak in and attach myself to the line without being seen. But no, old hawk eyes caught sight of me. It was the moment I had feared. I had seen other children cry out as the thick leather belt was brought down from high above on to the palm of their hand. Now it was my turn to face the executioner. I slowly walked forward, my feet heavy as lead weights, my heart thumping like kettle drums, all eyes staring at me. When I reached the front of the line, I turned my face away and closed my eyes as the belt came down with a crack. Then it was over, but I barely felt it. The fear of receiving the punishment was far worse than the actual lash itself. But I didn't ever want to go through that torment again. So from then on I made sure I was never late or dared to do anything wrong at school.

The school was a big timber building on two floors with a staircase on the outside leading to the upper floor. The classrooms were separated by wooden partitions. In front of the rows of wooden desks was a large blackboard, and next to it was the teacher's desk. We were never allowed to speak in class unless spoken to. Everyone had great respect and admiration for the teachers who were firm but friendly, they stood for no nonsense. Most had dedicated their lives to teaching and their expectations of us were very high. We were taught the British way, the 'three

Rs': reading, writing and arithmetic because it was considered to be the best education in the world. As we were colonised and ruled by Britain before the island became independent, all out textbooks came from England and were precious to us.

Each morning, before schoolwork we would have to sing 'God Save the Queen', 'Rule Britannia' and 'Land of Hope and Glory'. We were encouraged to feel proud that we were British, and even celebrated British memorial days like Remembrance Day. The poppies looked striking on our royal blue uniforms.

Every day we went through the ritual of saying our times tables; the whole class reciting as one. I can still hear the sing-song chanting in my ears. Occasionally the headmistress would randomly single out an unsuspecting pupil and ask them to repeat their tables. You never knew when it would be your turn so you had to be sure you knew them all by heart. It must have worked because I've never forgotten mine. We also learned about Britain and how the British conquered the world. We learned about the heroes of British history, and other countries in the world, but nothing about our own people. We even learned about British poets. My favourite was Alfred, Lord Tennyson, and at the age of six I could fluently recite his poem 'The Beggar Maid'. I can still remember the first lines: 'Her arms across her breast she laid; She was more fair than words can say . . .'

The best time at school was break-time. The recess bell would go and we would file out into the school yard in an orderly way, but once we were outside, we would let rip. It was time to let off the pent-up energy, time to shout, scream, laugh and play with our friends.

Skipping and hopscotch were two of my favourite games as well as action and clapping games to which we would sing 'Brown Girl in the Ring' and 'I Am a Pretty Little Dutch Girl'. I also used to look forward to seeing the woman who sold treats. She sat on a stool with a tray in front of her laden with goodies. Pink and white sugar cake, which was grated coconut, sugar and colouring; tuloons – a mixture of grated coconut and molasses; chana – fried chickpeas; spicy marinated mangoes, and snowballs, which were crushed ice covered in fruit syrup, all on sale for a few cents. The worst part was that I could never decide which to have, and I sometimes wished break-time would go on forever so I could try them all.

At lunchtime, everyone went home to eat as most of our mothers always stayed at home and very rarely went out to work. Sandra and I would hold hands and walk back home, always on the right side of the busy main road because the cars drove on the left, just as they do in England. We had to be careful as we walked along, because there were no pavements and the big American cars, single deck buses and wooden trucks were always driven far too fast along the narrow tarmac roads. An hour after one of Marmie's delicious hot cooked meals we were on our way back to school for afternoon lessons. Sometimes we would have nature classes, in which we learned about insects, birds and flowers. I remember the fascination of discovering how a chrysalis turns into a butterfly. For days we watched and waited to see the transformation; when it came it was like a miracle. I marvelled at the sight of the delicate, brightly coloured newborn creature. I treasured the moment and it is locked away in my mind, together with all the other unforgettable memories of my early school days.

Chapter Three

Celebrations

The biggest celebration we had at our house was for my baby sister Cynthia's christening. I was seven at the time, so old enough to look after Lester, Ellington and my two-year-old baby brother Roy (actually we called him Junior because Roy was also my father's name, which was quite a common thing to do in Trinidad). Marmie had got up early to prepare the food: curry chicken, rotis, souse (marinated pig's trotters with cucumber), peas and rice, exotic drinks and ice cream. She had done all the baking the night before and had made a special cake for Cynthia which was iced and decorated with pink flowers.

When it was time to go to church for the christening ceremony, baby Cynthia was dressed in a beautiful white cotton and lace gown which had been passed down. Sandra was the first to wear it so now it was on its sixth outing. That was one of the few things Sandra ever got to wear new because, even though she was the eldest, she was also the smallest so she got all the hand-downs. I got the new dresses and shoes which were always passed down to her and she used to complain bitterly about this. After the ceremony the four godparents, along with family and friends, came back to our house to eat, drink and celebrate the baby's health. It was customary to give the baby a gift, usually silver, a coin or a small trinket like a bracelet and Cynthia got lots.

Dardie played the saxophone in his spare time. He played music at dance halls at weekends for weddings, dances and parties. But today he and some friends played music on the gallery for his daughter's christening. I loved the music and took great delight in showing everyone the latest dance.

I remember our Christmas celebrations, too. This was another time for feasting. It was the only time of the year we had apples – big, red, juicy, crisp ones. They were one of the special treats we had at Christmas time, along with ham and a rich rum fruitcake. We didn't have

Christmas trees or snow but I would imagine what it would be like by looking at the Christmas cards which came from England and America. We all sang carols at special services and got presents which were usually clothes and books. One year Marmie bought us all expensive toys – dolls, cars, spinning tops – but by Boxing Day we had broken them all, so she vowed never to buy us toys again and she kept her promise.

We celebrated most of the British holidays. Bank holidays were usually spent by the seaside. I loved it when we went to the beach up north at Couva and Chaguanas. Marmie would pack a large picnic and we would sometimes take a train to get there: small wooden carriages pulled by a steam engine which clacked along the narrow lines. We would sit excitedly on the wooden slatted seats and as soon as we left the station we would ask Marmie if we were there yet. The train departed from San Fernando and we would pass by the huge oil refineries, with pipelines leading in every direction making it look like a picture in a science fiction comic. We could also see the pitch lake where the mountains of tar waited to be transported around the world. We would pass

through small villages which were next to sugar cane fields and coconut groves. We could see workers knee-deep in the rice paddy fields picking the grain in the hot sun. Dozens of tropical birds, such as salmon-pink ibis, would take off from the bird sanctuaries on the rivers as the noisy train rattled past. The cows and the goats would look up dismissively at us in the carriages as they grazed on the hillsides.

The journey took its time but was never boring. Passengers could move from carriage to carriage by walking along the narrow ledge on the outside of the train. This was exciting to watch but very dangerous and we were never allowed to try it. Musicians often played on the train and people would dance in the aisles, even the children. Everyone knew how to have fun. When we got to the beach we couldn't wait to strip down to our costumes and dash madly into the warm, blue, inviting Caribbean sea. After we had worked up an appetite swimming and splashing about we would sit on the golden sand and eat our picnic. Some people even cooked on the beach in cast iron pots over hot coals. The sizzling of fried chicken, rotis, curry and roast corn left a mouthwatering aroma in the air which mixed with the salty sea breeze. Sometimes men would come round selling coconut water. They would slice the top off a coconut, still in its outer green husks and sell it for a few cents. We had to share one amongst all six of us, and the juice often dribbled down our faces onto our necks, but we didn't care – we would wash it off in the refreshing tropical sea.

Carnival is the celebration for which Trinidad is famous. It is held three days before Lent, although preparations for carnival take a whole year.

The biggest parade took place in Port of Spain, the bustling capital of Trinidad. Some of the houses there looked like Scottish castles made out of wood. There was a very strong British, Spanish and French influence in the architecture which came with the people who colonised the island over the years. There

was a huge park called The Savannah where the big
carnival ended up after the people and floats had
paraded through the streets. This was called 'playing
mas'. We usually stayed in Marabella to watch the
people 'play mas' on their way to San Fernando,
the next biggest town. Some of the costumes were
fantastic. Each one would have a different theme, like
the undersea world, the galaxy, the animal kingdom,
birds or flowers. My first memory of carnival was
not a nice one though. I remember someone in a
bizarre towering monster costume dancing up to me.

It was a frightening sight, and I screamed in terror, ran into the house, and hid under the bed. It was only as I grew older, I appreciated more and more the spectacular, colourful carnival extravaganza, and like all Trinidadians every year I looked forward to singing calypsos and dancing, or 'jumping up' as we would say, to the steel band music.

Chapter Four

Darkness and Light

There were usually two kinds of weather on our tropical island, which was not far from the Equator: hot or rainy. When it was hot, from October to June, it was very hot. In the mornings we would wake to brilliant blue cloudless skies with a bright yellow sun beating down on us. The only relief was the occasional cool breeze that drifted in from the sea. You couldn't move fast in the heat, so everything was done at a slow pace. You could feel the heat coming through the soles of your feet as you walked along. People would often stop and stand idly on street corners chatting while they wiped away the sweat.

The ground was dry and dusty and the tarmac roads sometimes used to melt. The smell of the tar was overpowering as the traffic drove over the black, gooey mixture leaving their tyre marks in it. By midday the heat haze shimmered high off the hot ground, the sun baking everything in sight, forcing people to look for some shade away from the furnace-like heat. Mercifully at round about five o' clock it began to grow cooler. Then a sudden darkness would fall as the sun dropped out of sight below the horizon where it would slumber until the next morning. The darkness came so quickly after the light, it was like someone turning off a switch. But you could always be certain the sun would rise gloriously again and again during the hot season.

I loved the sun because the heat warmed my inner soul and gave me a free, happy, relaxed feeling. I also got a good feeling when it rained – and when it rained, it really rained. The heavens would open and torrents of rain would lash down. We would dance and splash in the warm, tropical scented water. It didn't matter if we got wet because, after the downpour, the water would evaporate in no time, drying our clothes in an instant.

It rained most heavily in the mountainous, tropical rainforest area where the land crabs, toucans, exotic parrots, huge toads and snakes lived, and where fragrant lilies, orchids and other vibrantly coloured flowers grew. Here the trees were immensely tall, exceptionally green and lush with thick vines entwining themselves around the trunks. The sun rarely got through to the dense undergrowth but the rain did.

Some of my cousins lived up there and near their house was a waterfall. We carefully used to make our way to it from their back yard, across the boulders and stones, pushing aside the branches and vines which hung down. We could hear the rushing water tumbling over the rocks and would shriek with delight as we stood under the cool water which felt like silk on our skin.

One day I remember experiencing weather like I had never seen before. One minute there was brilliant sunshine, the next a great darkness enveloped the island. At the same time the ground trembled, causing cracks to appear under my feet. A water pipe erupted, flooding the main street. I really thought the world was going to end and I screamed for my mother in terror. She told me it was freak weather, an eclipse and a slight earthquake happening, amazingly, at the same time. She held me tight and told me that it wouldn't last long. I was only seven years old and I didn't fully understand at the time what was happening. All I knew was that my little world looked and felt different. Then an almighty downpour of rain started to fall and for once I didn't dance in it.

Chapter Five
The Baptism

When you are six or seven years old and are made to go to church regularly, it can seem as if you are there for most of your life. Every Sunday morning Marmie would dress us in our Sunday best: starched cotton dresses with puffed sleeves, white socks worn with freshly whitened sensible shoes, and hair pulled back in tightly plaited bunches, decorated with brightly coloured ribbons, which all went together to give us that 'Sunday best' feeling. Perhaps that's why I still love dressing up today! When she finally got all six bickering and excited children ready, which was quite a feat, we would go to early morning service at the local Pentecostal church. The preacher there was a huge tall man – he looked as tall as the church, especially when he stood on the pulpit. I thought he was a giant! His skin had a rich, dark, ebony sheen; it was truly black! His expressive eyes shone like a torch when he spoke to us and you wouldn't dream of not paying attention, even though sometimes it was hot and uncomfortable. The women always brought fans with them which they would wave continuously as they shouted 'Hallelujah' every now and then.

At a certain point during the service the children would go to a room off the main part of the church. There we would have our own special service and be told Bible stories that taught us how to care for each other. We had to recite the ten commandments and say prayers for our families and friends. I always had a good feeling inside when I said my prayers. It was a contented feeling of happiness, and of understanding the difference between right and wrong.

You would have thought that all this was enough church-going for one day, but no. After lunch Marmie would take us to the Salvation Army Sunday school. I loved going there because, apart from all the singing and praying, we were taught to play musical instruments. Even though I was not much of a musician, I was a hit on the triangle and cymbals –

just one note at a time though. All of us together must have sounded dreadful but it was great fun and it was a good way of letting off steam.

The weekly ritual still didn't end here. At six o'clock we would finish off at the local Anglican church for evening service. Although I was christened in the Anglican church, my parents took us to most of the other churches, as they thought it was important that we understood and appreciated how others worshipped. They felt it would give us a broader outlook on life. But the places of worship that intrigued me most, even though I never got the opportunity to venture inside, were the Hindu temples, of which there were many in Trinidad. I always wondered what went on inside those beautiful buildings, especially when they were all lit up with hundreds of twinkling candles during Diwali, the festival of lights.

Out of all the services I did attend, I remember the ones from the Pentecostal church most of all because those were the most uplifting. The rejoicing from the congregation almost raised the roof. I used to watch open-mouthed, fascinated by the women who trembled and shook their bodies in the aisles as they felt 'the spirit'.

One Sunday, instead of going to church we all went to a river to see a baptism ceremony. Everyone was dressed in white: the women and girls in long flowing dresses with white scarves wrapped as turbans on their heads, the men and boys in white shirts and trousers. The tall preacher man looked more gigantic than ever as he stood at the water's edge. He spread out his arms, looked up to the sky and prayed for the souls of the people to be blessed. Then he called forward all those who wanted to be baptised and one by one, after a prayer with each, he ducked them under the water three times. They came out drenched but rejoicing, all except the children who seemed a little overwhelmed by the whole experience. The spirit of the baptism was intoxicating, the smell of the ointment used tantalised my nostrils. The mood of the men, women and children, all bare-footed and chanting, is embossed on my memory.

Chapter Six

Coming to England

There was always talk of someone who had left the island, who had gone to England to be met with open arms. Fantastic stories of how life was wonderful and how much money could be made; of how the islanders were wanted and needed to help Britain build herself up again in the years after the war, and how people could better themselves overnight. The streets were said to be paved with gold. Life was far from unbearable in Trinidad but many people were tempted by these stories and couldn't resist the opportunity. Not only unskilled workers but artists, writers, musicians, students, as well as assorted intellectuals made the decision to leave their tropical island home.

As children we didn't take much notice of all this talk. It was almost like the stories Dardie had made up for us. But all of a sudden the stories got very close to home. While in bed one night Sandra and I overheard Dardie telling Marmie that he wanted to go and make a new life in England. He was frustrated by not being able to play jazz, the music he had heard so much about but got such little opportunity to play because the music in Trinidad was calypso, Latin and steel pan. A friend who had settled in England had written and told him he could not only get a chance to play jazz but also make lots of money. The discussion went on into the night, and over the following weeks newspapers advertising jobs and boat journeys to Britain were left around the house. Some nights, in bed, I could hear Marmie crying, saying she would never leave us. I felt so reassured by those words, they were my only comfort during those restless nights. I started to have dreams, bad dreams, nightmares of being left alone, falling with no one to catch me. I told not a soul about my dreams and anxieties – if I did then perhaps they would come true and I didn't want them to. So I kept silent, pretended I didn't know what was going on. But the talk of going to England never stopped.

Then finally it was decided that all eight of us couldn't go at once, so Dardie would go first and send for us later. I was so relieved that Marmie wasn't going to leave us too. I was sad to see Dardie go, so I cried a little when he left, but was soon back to my old self. Life hadn't changed much as Marmie was still with us, things were almost back to normal, no more constant talk of going to England. But then the unthinkable happened: Marmie started asking family and friends if they would look after us, because she was going to join Dardie in England without us. I was devastated; she was going to break her vow, she had said she would never leave us.

I wished night after night that it wouldn't happen. I thought my wish had come true when none of my family would take us – they all had too many children. Grandparents usually took care of the children when parents left for a new world but that was not to be the case with us, we had none. Marmie began to sell the furniture and all her jewellery as well as the silver we got for our christenings. She started singing in her own special way. The same song she sang before Dardie left – now she was singing it again and again:

'This is the hour when we say goodbye,
Soon you will be sailing far across the sea
When you're away please remember me.'

She would start to cry and hug us while she sang. Then we would all start to cry. I couldn't understand why she wanted to leave us. If she loved us why couldn't we all stay together, especially as no one wanted to take care of us?

But she kept telling us that she did love us and that is why she was going to England to try to make a better life for us. We couldn't all go together because she and Dardie didn't have enough money, but one day they would.

Unexpectedly two of our godparents said they would take us. We couldn't stay together though. Lester and Ellington would stay south in San Fernando, Sandra and I would go north to Tunapuna. The lucky two were Cynthia and Junior, the two youngest, who would go

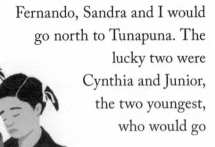

with Marmie to England. This was the day when a veil of unhappiness came down on my life. To be separated from Dardie was bad enough, he had now been gone for a year. But to be separated from my beloved Marmie and my younger brothers and sister was like the end of the world to me. My happy little world was beginning to crack and break into pieces, drifting away from me like flower petals scattered on a pond. We were all so very close, we all played together and had no other friends. Life was going to be sad and lonely and that soon proved to be true.

The people who looked after Sandra and me (we called them Auntie and Uncle as a sign of respect even though we weren't related) treated us like servants. Lester and Ellington were treated even worse by the people who looked after them. They had to fight each other for food, winner take all. They worked hard in the day and at night were forced to sleep not in a bed but under it! We were told every day that we were lucky to have someone to give us a home and that we should be grateful to them because we could have ended up in an orphanage. Later Marmie told us that twice a month she had sent us money, clothes and parcels but we never saw any of them.

Instead, we had to work from five o'clock in the morning cleaning the house, preparing meals and washing, all before we left for school. I was so tired I didn't learn much at our new school. But I remember Sandra and me being bullied because we were newcomers. I was a good fighter and fought Sandra's battles for her too.

One of the most embarrassing moments I had there was when the elastic in my home-made knickers snapped as I ran to school to avoid being late. The knickers landed at my feet and all the children started laughing at me, especially one particular boy. I was so angry and humiliated that I lashed out at him. He was bigger than me, but I didn't care. I must have looked and acted crazy because from then on no one ever laughed, teased or bullied Sandra and me again.

After school it was no fun, except when we walked home during the mango season. The mango trees would be laden with ripe juicy fruit. It looked so tempting and irresistible that Sandra and I would risk all to get some of the sweet, mouthwatering fruit. We would climb over the fence and pick as many mangoes from the drooping branches as we dared before the owner chased us off. If the mangoes weren't ripe we would both get tummy ache from eating them.

One day, on our way home, we saw the preparations for a funeral. A local man had died and neighbours were encouraged to go in and pay their last respects. Sandra and I persuaded each other to go in and pay ours. I didn't know what to expect or quite understand why I was going in; the truth was that I didn't want to go home and anything to delay us for just a blissful moment was welcome. So we shuffled into the hushed room where the open mahogany casket was laid on the table. I slowly edged forward until it was my turn to say goodbye. I looked down at the old man's face and was so surprised at what I saw. It was the most peaceful and serene face I had ever seen. He didn't look old and wrinkled but contented, almost smiling. I smiled back at him as I whispered goodbye under my breath. I wasn't scared, but happy that I had discovered something that, up until then, had been the unknown. The atmosphere at the funeral was quite different. This was when the mourners let their feelings out – they cried and wailed, some even threw themselves across the casket. Later that evening the family had a 'wake' to celebrate his life and give him a good send-off. It was like a party.

There was nothing for me to celebrate when I got home, only work: ironing clothes, picking the husks off the rice, sweeping the big dusty yard and collecting the eggs. I remember once having to catch a chicken, wring its neck, pluck the feathers and prepare it for dinner. I hated doing it and cried myself to sleep that night. In fact most nights Sandra and I cried

ourselves to sleep. We wrote to Marmie in England but our letters were always vetted and lines crossed out if Auntie and Uncle didn't approve of what we wrote. After a few months we moved to a new house with an inside bath and toilet. Auntie bought all the latest gadgets: a fridge, an electric iron – you name it, she bought it. She was a very superstitious woman and each day at the new house Sandra and I had to go through the bizarre ritual of waking up at four in the morning and sprinkling holy water around the house, especially across the doorway, to ward off evil spirits.

I couldn't understand why we had to do this as we were being treated in an evil way inside the house. To me the evil had already entered. It felt as if our sentence of unhappiness was going to last forever. I prayed and wished for the day when I would be with Marmie, Dardie and all my brothers and sisters again, for the happy, carefree days of family life which gave me such a feeling of security and confidence. I had lost that feeling and longed to get it back.

Chapter Seven

The Last Goodbye

Out of the blue – actually it was fifteen months after Marmie had left – we got a letter telling us she had made arrangements for all four of us to join her in England. It was during the August school holidays and Sandra and I hugged and danced for joy. Our prayers had been answered. We were on our way to being one big happy family again.

The time leading up to our departure was a hive of activity. We had two weeks in which to pack and say goodbye to everyone. Auntie and Uncle started being really nice to us. I suppose they wanted us to tell our parents how good they had been to us. This wasn't true, of course, but I forgave them; I would forgive anyone anything because I was so happy. I couldn't sleep at night, I was too restless with excitement. At that

moment in time I had no sad thoughts about leaving my country behind, even though I might not see it again for a very long time. Nothing occupied my mind and thoughts except being part of a family again.

Finally the day for our journey across the ocean came. My mother had asked her sister Olive to buy the tickets for all four of us. Auntie Olive lived in Port of Spain which was where we had to board the ship for England. We spent our final night with her before being packed into her car for the drive through the busy evening traffic to the port. I had been there before to wave goodbye to Dardie when he left the country. But now it was my turn to leave these tropical shores for the first time in my life. I was just about to begin a journey of a lifetime which would take fifteen days across 4,000 miles of ocean.

The excitement at the port gave me a tingle inside. I felt butterflies in my tummy. I could see the big ship far out in the water. It couldn't come right up to the side of the wharf because the water wasn't deep enough so everyone had to be transported to the ship in small motorboats. There was so much

noise it was deafening, everyone was pushing and shoving, people were shouting, making sure their trunks and suitcases were safe as the boats ferried backwards and forwards. I felt bewildered, lost amongst the other passengers and those who had come to bid them farewell. Many were hugging and crying as they said goodbye. Prayers were being said for a safe passage. Suddenly I started to cry too. I felt scared, but of what I wasn't sure. Perhaps it was because I now realized what was about to happen. I was leaving my homeland, the land where I had experienced great happiness with my family. Maybe it was because I was frightened of going into the small boat as it bobbed on the dark, oily water – water which crazily reflected the harsh harbour lights like a liquid mirror and separated us from the waiting ship that seemed to be calling me to her. Maybe I was just scared of facing the unknown. I still don't know.

Eventually I managed to get into the boat after being coaxed along with Lester, Ellington and Sandra. We all held on to each other tightly and just about managed to wave to Auntie Olive before the roar of the engine drowned out our goodbyes. She looked smaller and smaller as the boat left the quayside and neared the enormous ship. I became even more anxious as I realized that we were on our own, four young children without anyone to reassure, comfort and protect us. My thoughts were interrupted as the boat bumped against the side of the ship, alerting me to another challenge that loomed in the shape of a shaky rope ladder on the side of the ship which we had to climb. I really thought I was going to fall into the deep dark water. My heart thumped and my knees went weak but, encouraged by the sailors, I made my way up the ladder. At last I reached the waiting hands of the sailors who hoisted me on to the deck. I had made it.

Everyone was on board and I heard the loud

clanking sound of the anchor being winched up. A thundering noise bellowed out of the huge ship's funnel and we started to move, slipping gently and quietly into the darkness. I'd never been out of the country before but as I stood on the deck of the ship that was about to take me on the longest journey of my life, I smiled. This was the beginning of my great adventure, my new life.

I turned and looked back at the port lights twinkling in the distance. I looked for the last time at Trinidad and said a silent goodbye.

Chapter Eight
Life at Sea

The big Spanish ship, which had already picked up passengers from Grenada and Barbados, was like a floating skyscraper with stairs, numbers, letters and arrows pointing in every direction. On our ticket was a number and a letter which were called out and we were told to gather together with the rest of the passengers with similar numbers. We were then taken down into the belly of the ship to a tiny cabin with two bunk beds and a sink in the corner. Our cases were already piled up under the small porthole. This was to be our home for over two weeks. We climbed into bed, exhausted, and fell fast asleep.

The next morning I woke up feeling as if someone had beaten me over the head. I felt dizzy and nauseous. I had never had this feeling before. Sandra said she felt the same. We both rushed to the basin to be sick. The only relief was to stay in bed or to crawl up to the deck and stand perfectly still while breathing in the sea air. I remember being given tomato soup and corn puffs to eat which, I was told, would make me feel better but they only made me even more sick. I still can't stand the sight of either. This was a disappointing start to my adventure, not the way I had expected it to begin.

The seasickness lasted for about four days. On the fifth morning I felt surprisingly better. My body and head had got used to the ship's motion. I had gained my sea legs. Sandra still hadn't completely discovered hers. She had been given the responsibility of looking after us and making sure we behaved. Lester and Ellington and I tended to be a little wild in celebrating our new-found freedom and our antics made her anxious, but we weren't at all sympathetic to her predicament. We made a terrible noise and ran all over the crowded ship exploring all three decks, including the shaded one where many of the passengers sat relaxing, reading and playing cards.

We discovered every nook and cranny on board the ship and sometimes went into places we shouldn't have, even deep down in the two cargo holds which were packed with goods bound for Europe.

There were many other children who were

enjoying the freedom of the ship and some, like us, had no adult supervision. Even though Marmie had paid the shipping company for someone to keep an eye on us, no one ever did. As a result sometimes things got out of hand. One day Ellington had a fight with another boy on the deck. It started off as a rough and tumble, then it began to get out of control and, while Sandra and I pleaded for them to stop, they rolled closer and closer to the edge of the deck, nearer to the guard rail. I thought they were going to fall into the deep Atlantic Ocean. Suddenly from

high above a voice called for them to stop. It was the Captain who was watching the fight from his bridge. The last thing he wanted was children overboard. But the fight still kept going. Ellington was not the sort of boy to give in. The helmsman heeled the ship sharply over, which made us feel disorientated, but still the fight kept going. Then the Captain himself came down from the bridge and dragged the boys on to the deck just as they were about to fall in. He warned them both that if they couldn't behave they would have to stay in their cabins for the rest of the voyage.

The experience was frightening and shook us all, so after that the atmosphere and the journey became a little more controlled and we behaved less dangerously although we were still adventurous.

One evening at sunset, when the sea looked like waves of liquid gold, we saw the most amazing sight. Suddenly, as if by magic, the sea erupted with hundreds of arched shapes which dived back into the water. None of us had ever seen anything like it before. Then we realized that it was a shoal of flying fish, dancing and skipping across the ocean.

We watched the glittering spectacle until the sun died down and disappeared below the horizon.

We became friends with the Spanish sailors who cooked the meals down in the galley. There were hundreds of passengers on board to be fed and plenty of food to prepare. Mountains of potatoes had to be peeled everyday and the sailors entrusted us with that duty. At the time we thought this was because we were their friends. It was only later that I realized they only had us around because we were doing their job for them! Each day a diet of soup, tasteless meat or fish with little flavour and potatoes was served up. Although we helped prepare it, we didn't eat it: I think we mostly lived on bread, water and canned fruit – the only food we found edible.

The adults all seemed to enjoy being on the ship. They were always laughing and having fun. For them it was like being on a cruise. They were all accustomed to working hard for a living and for two weeks they had all the food, drink and nightlife they wanted. At night, we used to sneak up on deck in our pyjamas and watch them dancing in the ballroom to the music. Many of the sailors also joined in with the socialising in the evening. One night we saw one of our sailor friends hugging and kissing a lady while they were dancing. We stared wide-eyed and drop-jawed at them for a while as they smooched together. We then giggled and ran back to our cabin with our secret.

We left behind the hot tropics and entered the warm Mediterranean where we stopped off in Spain. The sailors unloaded some of the cargo that the vessel was carrying. As we watched from the deck, I overheard some of the adults saying they wished that they could go ashore to see what Spain was like. That's how I knew it was Spain.

No one on board really wanted the voyage to end. It was a passage in time, laden with freedom and happiness, free of care and responsibilities. We were journeying towards the unknown. We all had romantic visions of what it was going to be like in England but still didn't want this part of our adventure to end. To tell the truth I hadn't thought of Marmie,

Dardie or of seeing my brother and sister in England since the start of the journey. It was only two or three days after we left Spain that these thoughts entered my head. Now everyone started talking about the 'big arrival' and a buzz of excitement was going round the ship.

I knew we were getting closer to England because the weather started to get much, much colder and the sun seemed to disappear under the low clouds. Marmie had written and told us that the place we were coming to was not as hot and sunny as in Trinidad. I now knew what she meant. Still, we kept warm by running around the ship frantically (walking never occurred to us). The day before we arrived there was an announcement that told everyone to pack their belongings; nothing was to be left behind. We didn't have much so it didn't take us long. That evening after dinner there was a big party at which everyone celebrated the end of the voyage. Life at sea was coming to a close but the memories of coming to England would linger forever.

Chapter Nine

Land Ahoy

On 1st September 1960 I woke to the sound of seagulls. Watery morning light flooded through the porthole. We had gone to bed late the night before, after all the party revelling, so we were a little slow in reacting that morning. As always, Sandra was the first out of bed. 'I can see England!' she shouted. The rest of us scrambled up and pelted to the porthole. She was right, there was land ahoy. I couldn't see much of it but it didn't matter. It was England, we had arrived. What joy!

We hugged and danced around the cabin; our dreams were coming true. The first thing to do was to make ourselves presentable for our arrival. We ran to the communal shower room and washed at breakneck speed. Marmie always told us it was essential to have a fresh body and clean underwear, especially on important occasions. Today was one of the most important of our lives. I plaited Sandra's hair and my own. I was always good at plaiting, even at an early age, and on this occasion I plaited her hair extra special and decorated it with ribbons just like Marmie would have done. We had had beautiful dresses made for us which we put on proudly, together with white shoes, socks and gloves. Lester and Ellington looked dashing in their brand new outfits too.

We all looked quite regal, no prince or princess could have felt better. By now the packed ship had made her way up the English Channel and was gliding slowly up the the Solent towards Southampton. All the decks were crowded with a massive amount of luggage as well as our fellow passengers who, like us, were dressed in their finery: the men in their baggy-trousered and wide-shouldered suits with stylish trilby hats; the ladies spruced up in colourful dresses with masses of crinoline under the skirts – and of course hats and gloves were a must.

Arriving at the port seemed to take forever, the excitement was overwhelming and everyone began to get very anxious. Lester was convinced the land was an iceberg which we were about to crash into. Apparently someone in Trinidad had told him England was as cold as an iceberg, so the nearer and colder it got, the more convinced he became that this was true. Sandra and I did our best to comfort him but secretly we both felt anxious and nervous about what was ahead of us. We stood on the deck trembling with cold but also with a little fear. The anxiety grew greater as we travelled cautiously into the dock, passing dozens of terminal sheds. In front of some sheds cargo and passenger ships were moored close to each other along the quayside.

The docks were a hive of activity, nothing like the small shallow one we had departed from in Trinidad. There were cranes, cargo boxes and people everywhere. The terminal sheds were big barn-like buildings with long corrugated-iron roofs, which seemed to squat on the concrete wharf. In a few of the buildings we could see passengers who had arrived before us on other ships. Over and over I kept asking myself when was this floating vessel going to come to a rest? Surely it wouldn't take the whole day to dock. We seemed so close but yet so far.

At long last the ship appeared to be getting closer to the quay. I could see hundreds of faces looking up at us, trying to spot their loved ones. I looked desperately for Marmie, hoping I would recognize her lovely face amongst the crowd. Suddenly there she was, beaming with joy like an angel, waving frantically at us. She clutched her bosom and seemed to shake her head with a sigh of relief as if to say, 'thank goodness my children are safe'. Then she started to wipe away tears with her handkerchief and motioned us to stay where we were, which was not really a problem as the four of us couldn't move – we were too numbed with excitement. There was a man beside her who was not my father. I could see her talking to him and pointing us out. Eventually, when the ship was anchored, he came on board up the gangway. He made his way over to us and introduced himself. He was a social worker whose job it was to meet passengers as they arrived and help those who needed advice about how to get to their new destination. Not everyone had friends or family to meet them on arrival so the social worker was essential. He looked after us because Marmie was not allowed to come on board and as we were children travelling alone he took charge of us. He bundled all our luggage together and swiftly pushed past the other passengers, the four of us in tow behind him.

My heart pounded loudly like thunder as I climbed down the gangplank, this time not with fear but with joy as I ran towards Marmie. We all made a dash for her and hugged her. She squeezed us so tightly I felt I would break. The love and joy that passed through every bit of our bodies was overwhelming. I was at last in paradise, clutching Marmie. I never

wanted to be away from her again. When we finally broke loose from her she opened a bag and and took out something for each of us. 'I thought you might be a little cold,' she said, 'so I got these for you.' She handed me a powder-blue knitted Marks & Spencer's buttoned-fronted cardigan, embroidered with pink and yellow flowers. It was gorgeous; I adored it, my first English present. I squeezed it affectionately. I felt as if I had been sprinkled with magic dust and that all my dreams were coming true. I was back with my beloved Marmie at long last.

Chapter Ten

Land of Hope and Glory

I skipped out of Southampton Docks with my feet not quite touching the ground. My head felt light with excitement. As I dodged out of the way of the throngs of people I began to tell my mother all the news, my brothers and sister also talking at the same time. Marmie looked so happy and smiling, more beautiful than I remembered her. She told us Cynthia and Junior were waiting for us with a friend in London, Dardie was at work and he was not allowed to take time off from the garage where he worked as a mechanic during the day.

Nothing she said quite sank in, I was too elated. I hardly noticed anything around me. The first thing that registered, though, was the sight and sound of a grey metal train winding its way towards me. It travelled on a maze of lines that criss-crossed each other. As it came closer Marmie had to raise her voice to tell us to keep away from the edge. The engine roared and hissed as it came to a standstill. Heavy metal doors were opened and people clambered out onto the platform. This train was so unlike the smaller wooden ones back in Trinidad that I almost didn't recognize it as one. It stood there hissing and panting on its tracks, resting like an animal getting ready to pounce again. A loud distorted voice suddenly spoke and the sound nearly made me jump out of my skin. It was the announcer telling us that the train would soon be leaving for Waterloo.

We climbed onto the train excitedly and sat on the cushioned seats. Marmie told us we didn't have to clutch on to our luggage and she put our bags up on the racks provided. I felt like a princess, travelling in style. We all rushed over to the window as the train pulled out of the terminal building. As it started to build up speed, the noise got louder and louder and we could hardly hear ourselves speak, so I just gazed out of the window. All four of us had fought to get to the window seat but Marmie said we could each sit by a window in the small carriage. I gazed out breathlessly and tried to take in all the new sights.

The grass was so green, and so many different shades. The cows and the sheep looked like toys in the open fields. Some of the trees looked like the ones I had seen on Christmas cards. I felt as if I was in heaven. I looked over at Marmie, rushed to her and hugged her. I was so happy I could have cried.

The journey took nearly two hours and as we neared London the scenery changed dramatically. Rows and rows of red brick buildings with black slate roofs and smoking chimneys dominated the skyline. I had never imagined anything quite like this. The

houses had such a cold, lifeless look about them, not like the colourful, attractive ones I had left behind. But the sight of Waterloo station, standing there palatial and majestic with its numbered platforms stretching into the distance, convinced me that I was truly in England, the land I had loved from afar.

We finally stopped and carefully climbed down from the high carriage. I thought I would fall down the gap between the platform and the train and was relieved to feel solid ground beneath my feet. We gathered up our luggage and as we passed through the ticket barrier and wandered into the cathedral-like booking hall crowds of people started to swarm around us. They came from everywhere, carrying briefcases and umbrellas, wearing bowler hats, marching like ants, briskly and purposefully. Marmie told us we were in 'the rush hour' and to stay close to her as we made our way down a moving staircase. At first I thought I was experiencing another earthquake but Marmie reassured us that it was safe. Still I hung on tightly as the escalator took us deep underground to another kind of train. I was beginning to feel a little bewildered. It was all becoming too much to take in as we dodged the oncoming passengers along the narrow winding corridors. When we got to the platform we had to wait for a while for the train to arrive. Then all of a sudden out of the dark tunnel shot a train, as quick as an arrow. I jumped and panicked a little because the noise was so frightening and deafening.

I began to feel drugged on a cocktail of different sounds. New sounds that my head and body would have to get used to. Only my excitement kept me going. I had only been in England for six hours but I had experienced more than I thought imaginable.

Here I was travelling deep under the ground on a fast-moving train with automatic closing doors which made it feel as if I was travelling in space. None of us spoke but our eyes were open wide with amazement. Eventually we got to our stop. Marmie told us it was Turnham Green station. I saw it written up on the wall in big bold letters surrounded by the round blue, white and red symbol of the Underground. As we came out of the station the sunlight dazzled my eyes and the noise of the rush-hour traffic made me freeze like a scared rabbit.

My new world seemed like a fast-moving jungle as Marmie led the way home and we all trailed along behind her on the hard concrete pavements. It was the only safe place to be, away from the cars, heavy lorries and big red double-decker buses that sped along the wide roads. I sometimes had to run to keep up with Marmie because I had stopped to marvel at a shop window. I was also fascinated by the red pillar boxes that sat regally on some of the pavements and by the tall red boxes with glass windows and telephones inside. In Trinidad you had to go to the post office to post a letter or use the telephone – you couldn't do it anywhere and everywhere. England was certainly different, perhaps her streets were paved with gold, although I hadn't seen any yet!

I soon began to notice people staring at us. I thought it was because we were wearing brightly coloured clothes, our very best clothes. They all had on such dull, drab colours: black, navy and grey, as if they were going to a funeral. What I didn't realize was that staring was something I was going to have to get used to.

At last we turned into the road which was to be

our home for the next month: 1 Mayfield Avenue, a two-storey semi-detached red brick house with a brown door. I felt nervous and anxious as Marmie opened the door with her key. She led us up the narrow staircase and along a landing. Then she

unlocked another door. As she opened it she said, 'Welcome to your new home.' I slowly crept into the dark, dingy room and looked around. I took in the contents of the room: a double bed, table, couch, some chairs, cupboards and a wardrobe. Was this it? Surely this couldn't be what we had travelled thousands of miles for. Was I to start my new life living in this cluttered room? I felt a swell of disappointment rising inside. The whole day had left me emotionally drained and to crown it all I had ended up in one room which all of us would have to share. I hadn't considered the fact that it was all my parents could afford, that they had saved every penny to send for us to be together. All I knew was this was not what I wanted my new home to be. My dreams were shattered and scattered. I suddenly burst into hysterical tears. Sandra started to cry too, then the boys joined in. Nothing Marmie said could comfort us. She started to cry as well and began to prepare a meal. At least that was the one thing that hadn't changed – Marmie and her cooking.

Chapter Eleven
Settling In

It took us a few days to get over our disappointment and to adjust to living in the big city of London. During that time we got used to being with Junior and Cynthia again, who had both changed quite a lot. They had made so many presents for us at nursery school and also painted pictures of what they thought we would look like, which was most amusing. They had longed to be with us and asked so many questions about Trinidad and our adventurous voyage. They loved hearing the story of Ellington nearly falling into the ocean which got more and more exaggerated depending on who was telling the tale. The room was our playground and the noise we made inside those four walls was unbelievable. We were forever being told to be quiet, that we were not in Trinidad now where we could run free and play in the yard. Our new home didn't have a garden and Marmie would never allow us to play in the streets because it was far too dangerous.

One of the few times we were allowed to go outside was to collect the bottles of silver- and gold-topped milk left on the doorstep. At first I thought someone had left them as a free gift for us until I realised Marmie had to pay for the milk at the end of the week. In Trinidad, we used to buy milk from a man who came round on a bicycle with a small tank full of cow's milk on the back.

Marmie had made arrangements for us to go to a local school and after just ten days of being in England, I was on my way to my first English school.

When I arrived at the school, many of the children rushed over and touched me then ran away giggling. I thought they were being nice to me. At that time I didn't realize it was because I was different, a novelty, something to be made a fool of and to be laughed at. The dingy Victorian building squatted in the large grey playground like a bulldog ready to attack. It was surrounded by high wire fencing, a hopscotch game was marked out on the ground and on one of the walls a bull's-eye pattern was painted.

Above the school's main door were some letters engraved in the stone; they were Latin words and I

never did find out what they meant. Inside the school
the walls of the long corridors were tiled halfway up
making the building feel cold. The tiles had been
painted a mushy green, some of it flaking off where it
had been scratched over the years by passing children.
The ceilings and upper half of the walls were a
pale dull beige colour and the floors were covered
with worn and splintering wooden parquet. Off the
corridors were separate, unwelcoming classrooms,
each with its own door, not partitions like the ones
in Trinidad. But the desks and the blackboard were

the same. I felt a little comforted when I saw them. At least they were something I'd seen before.

The structure of the day was also a familiar routine: lessons, playtime, more lessons, lunch and play, then ending the day with more lessons. The work the teacher gave us was so easy and simple compared to the work I was used to. Yet the teacher treated me like an idiot because she couldn't understand my Trinidadian accent even though I could understand her. I felt like a fish out of water.

School took a great deal of getting used to, especially during the first few weeks. I found some things new and exciting – simple things like the taste of cold milk during the morning break. I would grip the small glass bottle tightly as I plunged the straw into the silver foil top and sucked out the creamy liquid. The only thing I wasn't so keen on was the thick, furry feeling it left in my mouth afterwards. There wasn't a stall selling treats in the playground but the children did play clapping and skipping games which made me feel at home. There was one game, however, which I didn't understand at first but in no time at all I began to hate. The first time I saw the children play it, I knew it was wrong and cruel. I was standing next to the wall with the painted bull's-eye when some boys came up and spat strange words at me, words that I had never heard before but from their faces I knew they were not nice words. They were words which told me I was different from them and that they felt my kind shouldn't be in their country. I looked at them, confused and baffled like a trapped, helpless creature. What was 'my kind' and why shouldn't I be in the country I was brought up to love? The land of hope and glory, mother of the free. I began to feel angry and violent as I stood and watched their ugly faces jeering at me. But they might as well have been talking in a foreign language because I didn't understand the words they were shouting. I didn't let them make me cry though, I had learned how to be tough during the time Marmie had left us in Trinidad. When I got home and asked Marmie what the words meant, she looked sad and sat us all down and slowly explained that because of the colour of our skin some people were going to be cruel and nasty to us. But we must be strong, make something of ourselves and never let them get the better of us. That was the day I realized that in the eyes of some in this world I was not a person but a colour.

I looked down at my hands and desperately tried to understand why my colour meant so much to some and disturbed them so deeply. In Trinidad there were people of all races, from all over the world, and they all lived together in harmony. No one felt threatened or was made to feel bad because of his or her colour. So why all the fuss in England? I felt so confused. A picture flashed up in my mind of Sandra and I holding hands and laughing as we skipped along Marabella main street to our friendly wooden two-storey school. Tears welled up in my eyes and I wished I was back there, happy and innocent again. For that was the day I had lost a certain innocence, and I would never be the same again. I, too, would now see a person's colour first and wonder whether he or she was going to hate me.

The next time the boys shouted racist words at me

they ended up against the wall. My battle for survival had begun. I was determined not to be the loser and I never was because Marmie told me over and over that no one was better than me and to be proud of who I was and of the colour of my skin. I liked myself and if anyone had a problem with my colour it was going to be their problem, not mine.

Chapter Twelve

Survival

The days and weeks turned into cold winter months and I felt as if my body was going to break. White steam came out of my mouth as I spoke. I blew on to my fingers to try to warm them but nothing could get rid of the tight, stiff feeling deep inside me. When we first arrived in England I thought it was cold but now I knew what coldness really was. Then, there was an orange-gold look about the trees but now it was freezing and the trees had lost their leaves so they stood naked like skeletons exposing every limb. I wished the cold grey misty mornings would go away for I longed to see the warm sun and feel the heat of it on my back, penetrating into my soul.

The wintry weather made me feel depressed. The nights seemed to start so early, even before the end of the afternoons. When we came out of school it was already dark. Once we came out and it seemed as if the world had disappeared under a grey blanket. I couldn't see anything except for fuzzy, distorted

lights coming at me out of the distance. People also started to appear from nowhere and disappear again. As I stumbled forward I squinted my eyes in an effort to see more clearly but it made no difference – the thick greyness was impenetrable. There was a hushed, mysterious feel to the atmosphere; even the usual traffic noise was muted as vehicles slowly crawled along the roads, creeping in and out of vision. The cold, sooty air seeped into my lungs and made me cough; it tasted horrible. Later on the radio I heard someone saying that it was one of the foggiest days London had ever seen.

In my short time in England I had experienced all kinds of unpleasant weather: cold winds that felt as if they would tear the skin on my face; freezing rain (not the sort I felt like dancing in); and days upon days without sunlight. I could never be sure what the weather would be like and I began to understand why the English always talked about the weather. There was so much of it.

There was, however, one kind of weather that made me feel happy even though it was cold. I so clearly remember the first time I experienced the thrill of it. On a cold morning, as I huddled under my thick blanket, the smell of the paraffin lamp still lingering in the air, I was awakened by a stillness, an eerie quietness. A strong, clear light shone through the curtains, not the usual murky greyness but a magical light. I sensed something was different about this day as I slowly went to the window. I lifted up the curtains and wiped the condensation off the pane. Then I saw it, a pure white blanket that dazzled me. It was a whiteness I had never seen before and everything was covered in it. I gasped with wonderment. The landscape looked so beautiful, it took my breath away. Surprisingly I didn't feel cold, the beauty had warmed me. I had fallen in love with snow. We spent the rest of the day watching from the windows. Marmie didn't send us to school because it was snowing, but she got told off by the headmistress who told her that next time we had to come to school in the snow – it would not hurt us, we would survive!

By the time spring came my feelings of uncertainty about my new homeland were beginning to thaw. Happier feelings began to blossom in my mind. Perhaps it was because suddenly everything in the land started to come alive again. The yellow daffodils popped out and waved like flags. Cherry blossom decked the bare branches in pink garlands. I hoped that suddenly people's feelings would open up towards me and blossom too.

I hated the rejection I had experienced so far. Even going shopping was an ordeal. Sandra and I would stand at the counter waiting to be served but would be ignored, treated as though we were invisible, and that hurt. Other West Indian children in my school had experienced the same hostility. We were treated without any respect and we were bundled together as coming from the same place. Our individual identity was never acknowledged. We had come from different islands – Jamaica, Barbados, Grenada, St Kitts, Dominica and Antigua – and spoke with different accents. We were brought up with different cultures and music. Each island in the Caribbean was as different as France is from Finland as Spain is from Sweden – even we had to learn to understand each other. I couldn't understand why English people knew nothing about our different countries while we knew so much about theirs. But they just didn't seem to want to know. I always found it exciting when I met someone from a different country as it expanded my knowledge of the world. I, too, was coming into contact with Jews, Italians, Africans and West Indians from other islands, but I didn't treat them as if they were worthless beings with no feelings. So many British people thought we had come from a land of coconuts and palm trees, huts and beaches, not realizing that our buildings, history and food had strong European influences. In fact, we probably knew more about British history and culture than most of them. My uncle, like so many other West Indians, had fought and died for Britain in the Second World War. Hundreds of West Indians had joined the Army and the Air Force, and had fought to protect Britain, to make her a safe place to live. Little did that generation of West Indians know that their gallant action was to go unrecognized and forgotten and that many of their descendants would have to go through a gruelling survival course on arrival in Britain, and be made to feel unwelcome and unwanted in the celebrated motherland.

I came to England feeling special, like a princess, but was made to feel like a scavenger, begging for a piece of what I thought was mine. I had been told that I was part of the British Empire. Was that a lie? My dreams and visions had been shattered but I was in England now and there was no turning back. I had to learn to survive.

Chapter Thirteen
The Big Move

We had moved from the one room in Chiswick to two rooms in Penge, South London. In Trinidad we had always lived in a house on our own so it was very difficult for my family to adjust to living in two rooms and with other people in the same house. It was the same for many West Indian families. We were not welcomed in some areas and were made to feel that way. There were often signs in windows which read 'No coloureds'.

Consequently, West Indians tended to congregate in certain parts of a town or city. The different islanders often settled in the same area. Jamaicans, the largest percentage of West Indians, flocked to the major cities like Birmingham, Liverpool, Manchester and Bristol as well as London. Trinidadians mostly lived in North and West London. My family were among the exceptions, as we ended up living in Beckenham in Kent. My father had come to England to play jazz and he had fulfilled his dream. He toured all over Europe and Africa, although he did have to work as a mechanic during the day to supplement his income because jazz musicians didn't make very much money. Marmie was determined that we would have our own house, not one that was shared with other tenants, which was usually the case. She, like other mothers, worked very hard and saved every penny she could. To save enough for a house would have taken my parents forever, so Marmie joined what was known as a 'su su' or 'partner' with other West Indian families. This was a group of people who each put a sum of money, say ten pounds a week, into a fund then each week one person would get all the money, and so it went on until everyone had their turn.

Within a year of arriving in Britain we were able to buy our first house, which was in Anerley, near Crystal Palace. When we first moved in the neighbours made us feel most unwelcome. They tried flooding the house by putting a hose through the letterbox. Then they tried to stink us out by putting dog mess through it. A few years later, when we tried to buy our house in Beckenham, the neighbours actually called the police to arrest us for trespassing. When we eventually moved in many of the neighbours moved out. This was quite a common reaction when any black families moved into an area where mostly white people lived.

All this was very painful to bear but Marmie always tried her best to make us forget the outside world. She used to encourage me to perform for family and friends, showing them the latest dance and singing while Dardie played the saxophone. Lester and Ellington took up musical instruments and accompanied us.

The one addition we thought our family needed to make us really happy was a pet. It was not easy trying to persuade Marmie to get us a dog or a cat though. We kept telling her how all the English children at school had pets, especially dogs, and what fun they seemed to have with them, treating them so lovingly. They would kiss them, keep them indoors, even sleep with them. I was quite amazed by all this because in

Trinidad dogs always slept outdoors and were treated like guard dogs, not like members of a family. The only pets that were kept inside the house were birds in a cage. My sisters, Sandra and Cynthia, kept on and on pleading with Marmie to get a pet and eventually she gave in. She bought us our very own pet, a rabbit. We called him Snowy and we treated him just like a dog. He would stand up on his hind legs and beg for food. Whenever we came home from school he would give us the biggest greeting ever. My brothers were given white mice as pets and they took great delight in scaring us girls with them by putting them in our beds at night. The boys thought this was highly amusing – but I didn't.

Another way Marmie thought she could keep us happy was by taking us on outings. We had some great adventures visiting the zoo, castles and museums. She would pack a huge picnic, buy Red

Rover return bus tickets and we would roam all over London and into the neighbouring countryside. Wherever we went people would stop and look with great admiration at my mother. She must have looked like a sergeant major giving her little army orders and there was never any question of us not obeying them.

She was a sort of Mary Poppins, keeping the six of us excited and amused but still under control. Once we had toured round London and the surrounding area, she decided that we should see other parts of England. It would have cost too much to go by public transport so she learned to drive and bought a second-hand Ford Zephyr. A few weeks after she had passed her driving test she packed us all in the car and headed north up the M1 to Leicester to see my uncle and his family. That was the first of many exciting car journeys. Sometimes we never knew where we were heading, but that made it all the more exciting. However, at Christmas time, on Boxing Day, we knew exactly where Marmie was taking us: she would drive us to the West End of London to see the lights in Regent Street. As we turned the corner of that famous street it was like entering a magical,

glittering wonderland. The decorative lights sparkled high above our heads and all we could say to greet them was 'ooh' and 'aah'. Then on to Trafalgar Square to see the giant Christmas tree that almost touched the sky. The excitement didn't stop there. The next stop was the Christmas party laid on for West Indian children which was always a happy occasion. That was where I met Santa Claus for the first time. I had heard so much about him and when he appeared carrying a huge sack, dressed in his bright red two-piece suit and hat with white fur trimmings, his white curly beard covering half of his smiling face, I knew it was him immediately. I couldn't wait to meet him – and get my hands on my present. A gush of excitement flooded through my veins that first time, and I got the same feeling of excitement every year when it came to that moment.

Chapter Fourteen

Double Identity

It's not easy having to live and exist in two cultures at the same time, but that's what I had to get used to. At school I had to adapt to the life of an English pupil. At least that's what I was told by a teacher a couple of years after I arrived. I still had a Trinidadian accent and I liked using it because it made me feel different, someone special amongst all the other South London accents spoken in the school. So I would put it on even stronger sometimes because it was something only I could do in the class and that made me feel good. One day the teacher who took us for English asked me to read a passage from a book, so I stood up and read in my most lyrical Trinidadian accent – but in mid-flow she shouted, 'Stop, you guttersnipe. If you want to stay in my class and be understood by everyone you will learn to speak the Queen's English.'

I was devastated. I was being told to give up the one special thing I had that made me feel good about myself at school. I started to cry, not because she called me a guttersnipe – she called everyone that – but because I was being stripped of my identity in front of the whole class. That day I couldn't wait to get home and tell my mother what had happened. Surely I would get some sympathy from her. But Marmie, like most other West Indian parents, wanted the best education for her children. West Indians were brought up to believe that whatever the teacher said was law. School was the place where lives could be changed for the better and social standards raised. So as far as Marmie was concerned I had to abide by the rules of the teacher. After that, every morning before we left home in our immaculate school uniforms, Marmie would line us up and tell us that we were in England now, we were to go to school and learn because our passport to life was our education. We were to make sure we took advantage of every bit of knowledge that was on offer. If we did so, no one would ever be able to take it away from us.

The next time I was asked to read for my English teacher I made an attempt to speak the Queen's English. Surprisingly enough it came quite easily because I knew I had a goal, to get the best education.

That was to be my reward and I wasn't going to let it slip away. I was the one who wanted the education that was on offer so I had to take charge of my destiny; if I didn't I would end up resentful. I didn't have to lose my identity either because when I got home I spoke in my natural tongue to my family. My beloved Trinidadian accent, with its rich tones, was not lost; I just had to learn to use it at the appropriate time.

West Indian children with strong accents, who could not be easily understood by the teachers, were banished to classes for children with special needs. As far as the teachers were concerned, if they could not understand what these children were saying then they considered them to be stupid – only good for the sports field. Many intelligent West Indian children left school under-achieving because no one, including the teachers, took the time to understand, nurture, guide or advise them like Marmie did for us.

School food was also a huge culture shock. The only time I didn't eat spicy food was when I had school dinners. I would line up in the noisy hall with the rest of the girls wondering what was going to be spooned on to my plate. The food always seemed to taste and smell the same, whether it was steak and kidney pudding, or Irish stew, and every dish was served with overcooked cabbage, lumpy mashed potatoes and soggy carrots. I always looked forward to the desserts, though. It didn't take me long to get used to Bakewell tart, rhubarb crumble, spotted dick and treacle pudding, all served with thick gooey custard.

I always knew it was Friday because fish and chips were served up with mushy peas. I soon learned that fish and chips were a part of British culture. Fish and chip shops always seemed to come alive at dusk when a welcoming orange glow and overwhelming frying smell would lure customers into the greasy white-tiled shrines. We very rarely ventured into them although they were a great talking point with most West Indians – not because of the thick batter coating that covered the fish or the greasy chips which were smothered in salt, but because we found it so amazing that the fish and chips were served in newspapers! Surely newspaper was for wrapping rubbish in, not for eating food from. I was pleased that at school we ate our fish and chips off a plate!

The food we ate at home was highly seasoned with dried herbs and spices similar to those used in the Caribbean. There were specialist shops where rice, the staple diet in the West Indies, exotic vegetables and fruits, spices and herbs were sold. These were very expensive because they were imported, but each week Marmie would visit these shops to buy the food we had grown up on. My father found it particularly difficult getting used to English-style cooking. Like most West Indian dads he always insisted on us eating West Indian food at home. I think it was because it was one of the few things that kept the Caribbean close to our hearts. The spicy flavours of Marmie's home cooking was always a great delight to the palette. She would serve up not only traditional Caribbean dishes but also anything from roast chicken to cottage pie, spaghetti bolognese to beef stew all cooked in her own inimitable West Indian style. Her cooking was part of the Caribbean culture of which I felt so proud – and still do.

There was one English custom at school that got me into deep trouble. It started off quite innocently in the playground at my school in Penge. I must have looked lost and alone because a group of children asked me to join in a game with them. One person was chosen to be 'it'. The rest had to run away and try not to get caught. This was a new game to me but I loved running and playing games so I was most enthusiastic and keen to take part. A boy called Norman was chosen to be 'it' and everyone ran off

squealing with delight and shrieking with laughter. I ran as fast as I could, dodging all the other children in the playground. But Norman was hot on my heels and eventually caught me. What happened next was most unexpected. He grabbed hold of me and kissed me full on the lips. No one had ever kissed me like that before, that sort of kissing was for grown-ups. I was so shocked by this display of passion that I smacked his face and gave him a black eye. Poor old Norman. In fact, it turned out to be poor old me. What I hadn't realized was that we were playing 'kiss and chase' and that Norman, the heartthrob of the class, had picked me to chase and kiss. All the girls had a crush on him and because he had chosen me, a newcomer, to kiss – and then to make matters worse I had beaten him up – they sent me to Coventry. Being sent to Coventry was another new custom, and an uncomfortable one, that I had to live with. I wondered if anyone would ever break the silence and speak to me again. To my surprise the first one to do so was Norman. What a nice guy he turned out to be. We became friends at school and often used to walk home together. But he never kissed me again.

Chapter Fifteen

Breaking Down the Barriers

If you belong to a large family you learn from a very early age to be extremely competitive. Belonging to our family was no exception. There was always a race to see who could finish first at almost anything: getting dressed, playing a game, answering a quiz or getting somewhere the quickest. Even mealtimes turned into a competition. This called for subtlety because Marmie was very strict about our table manners, but sometimes our manners went out of the window because of Junior's irritating eating habits. He had a small appetite and never finished all his food. The rest of us would be like crazed piranhas closing in, ready to gobble up any scraps left on the plate, and before he could say, 'I don't want any more,' his leftovers would be in one of our mouths and down the gullet. The winner was the champion of that sitting, and I won that challenge many times.

Being so competitive made me a high achiever at school, both academically and as an athlete. Exams were taken after crammed revision at the end of the school year and the results were always eagerly awaited at home. Everyone would be anxious to compare marks and passes. To get the most passes was great but to come top of the form was the ultimate prize.

The subjects I came top in were French, History, Geography, Maths and Music but I was lousy at Art. I was so bad that my art teacher, a real tyrant who we named 'Bulldog Burton', asked me to leave the class because my grades were so awful – Z minus! She wrote in my report that my 'enthusiasm would be better spent elsewhere'.

Some of that enthusiasm was spent competing in the sports arena, although I didn't use much of it in the swimming pool. This was because the teacher told me I didn't have to bother. She condescendingly informed me at my first swimming lesson that people of my race had an extra bone in their feet which made them unable to swim and if I tried I would sink immediately! So I was left on my own to splash and paddle around in the shallow end while the other girls were coached and encouraged to swim length after length from the deep end.

But I needed no encouragement when it came to netball, hockey, rounders and my greatest love, athletics. I adored all these sports and because of my great competitiveness I was usually the captain and champion of most of the teams. My enthusiasm drove my fellow teammates on. We played to win and if we didn't, I would make sure we did the next time. Motivating others was easy for me because at home it was a way of life. This competitiveness was a major plus on school sports day.

The big event was usually held on a hot summer's day in June. The smell of freshly cut grass lingered in the air as we marched out on to the carpet-like field. The perfectly straight, brilliant white painted lines on the green grass gave a feeling of formality. The noise of chattering, jittery schoolgirls grew louder and louder as the school emptied out on to the playing field. Dozens of girls in white aertex polo shirts and baggy navy blue knickers covered the horizon, each wearing a coloured sash representing her school house. I wore my yellow one proudly; I belonged to the house of Elizabeth Fry. The other houses were named after famous women too:

Florence Nightingale, represented by flame red; royal blue for Charlotte Brontë and emerald green for Edith Cavell. These women's names were on four boards in the great hall. Under them, listed by year, were the results of the winning houses and the names of the champions. Each morning as I filed into the hall for assembly I would pass the boards and hope that one day my name would be up there. On my first sports day I knew the opportunity had come for me to make that happen. This was my chance to show what I could do.

We sat cross-legged on the grass and waited for our names to be called out for our races. I heard my name called and walked to the starting line for the one hundred metres. As I crouched on my marks I could feel my heart thumping against my knee. I felt slightly dizzy and nauseous as I looked up my lane. Then I heard the loud bang of the starting pistol and saw the other runners pelting off leaving me frozen on the line. I managed to jerk my legs into overdrive and sped off too, clawing my way up the track, wind-assisted by my voluminous knickers, frantically reeling in runner after runner until I was out in front, pushing my chest towards the tape, breaking it with all my might. That was the first of my many victories at school. I felt so proud when I went up to receive my medal; the achievement meant so much to me. I later went on to represent the school in the county school championships. Our school usually won and it was customary for the captain to take the cup home, just for the weekend. When I became captain I looked forward to that privilege, but it was not to be. We did win and I did go up to receive the cup, but as I was about to go home with it, as my predecessors

had done many times before, the games teacher took it away from me, smiling falsely as she did so, saying, 'I'll look after that.' I handed the cup over in a state of shock, stripped of my privilege. I realized that she thought I was good enough to win races for them but not good enough to take the cup home to show my family. I was refused that honour. I walked home with my tears running down my cheeks, trying to think how I was going to explain my hurt and disappointment to my family.

They would help cushion the blow – not just Marmie but my brothers and sisters too. We all motivated each other and even though we fought like cats and dogs, no one from the outside world could come between us. My family was a source of strength, not just physical strength but spiritual strength. Marmie served up heaps of it to us each day and to top it up she also made sure that we went to church, just as we had done in Trinidad.

One Sunday morning we had all gone to a grey stone church in Penge to give thanks for what we had. Inside, the light from the stained glass windows shone on the handful of people taking part in the mild, controlled, unemotional service – not at all like the ones I was used to. Still, I said my prayers, asked for forgiveness and sang out as loudly as I could, trying to rejoice in the only way I knew how. At the end of the service we filed out, smiling and fulfilled. But as we stood at the top of the church's worn stone steps I noticed that the other parishioners looked tense and uncomfortable, not at all like people who had just come out from worshipping and whose souls had been rejuvenated.

I wondered why they looked so unhappy and angry. As we made our way down the steps and got closer to a group of them, I overheard words that I didn't expect to hear from so-called Christians. Instead of welcoming us to their flock they were saying, 'I see they are letting in that kind now. Is no place sacred?' Then it dawned on me – we were the only West Indians in the congregation, invading their little cosy world. I felt so betrayed. This was one set of people in England I expected to greet us with open arms but they proved to be totally hypocritical, going against everything they had just vowed to uphold: to love, care for and respect their fellow man and treat others as they would expect to be treated. We never returned to that church again, but instead went to a place of worship built by West Indians. That was the place where we were welcomed, where we worshipped and rejoiced, knowing in our hearts that we were wanted there.

Churches like this started to spring up all over the country and, whatever your needs, you could rely on them to help and support you, not only spiritually but in some cases financially as well. West Indian churches were always full to the brim with people rejoicing out loud.

I sang out, not only in church but at school too, where I took part in many competitions as a member of the school choir. The first time I performed a solo act was in the school Christmas concert. Up until then I had only performed at the concert with the choir but now I was going it alone. I took a while to decide what to do – act, sing or dance. I couldn't decide so I did all three! I chose the song 'She'll Be Coming Round the Mountain When She Comes' and dressed up as a hillbilly, complete with checked shirt, jeans, boots, hat and spotted necktie. I got the idea from one of the films I had seen back in Trinidad. I waited anxiously in the wings as the other performers carried out their routines. Then it was my turn. I was announced, the piano teacher played a loud intro and I was away. Something took over my body and I became a rootin', tootin' hillbilly, prancing energetically up and down the stage as if it were the Rockies! Thunderous applause broke my trance as I came to the end; everyone was screaming for more. The headmistress, Miss Bowles, a stout woman of vision, came on stage, shook my hand and congratulated me. She then asked the girls if they wanted to hear me again and they all shouted, 'Yes! More, more!'

I looked down at the sea of faces below me: they were staring back with a look in their eyes that I had never seen before; it was a look of admiration and respect. It seemed that suddenly they saw me as a person, not as a colour. I had no idea why it had taken a song-and-dance routine to change their perception of me, all I knew was that as I looked at them I could tell they saw me differently. Then I realized I had given the song everything and had overwhelmed them with my energy until their prejudices were swept away. At that moment I knew that in order to make a success of my life, be it as a doctor, a lawyer or a bank manager, I would have to work twice as hard as anyone else and be twice as good. I had to develop the ability to make people see me as a person, someone with feelings, pride, dignity and intellect. Dardie had opened our minds to the world with knowledge, Marmie had instilled strength, determination, conviction and confidence in us. Now it was up to me to merge them together and absorb them into my soul. These were to be the ground rules on which my new life was to be built. I had to make something out of it without losing my true identity. A massive task, but not an impossible one.

My thoughts were interrupted by the heavy notes of the piano playing the intro once again. This time I danced with joy for myself, revelling in my new discovery.

After the concert, in the playground, Sandra pushed her way though the throng of admiring girls and hugged me. She too had felt the barrier crumble. We had conquered them, a major leap had been taken that day. We were going to come up against more barriers in the future but there would be ways to break them down and with our competitiveness we could do it. I was convinced of that when someone from the crowd shouted, 'What are you doing at next year's concert?'

Sandra and I turned to each other and smiled, our eyes bright as moonbeams. Then we walked off home, hand in hand, eager to tell our news to Marmie and the rest of the family.

Afterword

Floella's sisters and brothers

I am often asked what became of my sisters and brothers? Well, Sandra joined an international pharmaceutical company and travelled the world. She promoted equality and diversity in the workplace and also became a school inspector for many years, as well as a volunteer charity worker. Lester qualified as an engineer and ended up being in charge of the upkeep of the Houses of Parliament Estates and received an OBE for his contribution. Ellington qualified as a quantity surveyor, became a property developer and ran his own construction company. Roy Jnr became a computer analyst and was part of the team that developed the barcode. He created the supermarket self-checkout system and helped develop numerous global IT products.

Cythia became a classical pianist, businesswoman and a top financial advisor.

The Legacy of the
Windrush Generation

Floella and her siblings made the two-week sea voyage from the Caribbean to England in 1960, to join their parents in London. Their journey was one that had been undertaken by many before them, as part of a movement of people who came to Britain after the Second World War in search of work and better prospects for themselves and their children.

After the War, Britain's workforce was left badly depleted, so the government encouraged people to come from other Commonwealth countries to fill the gaps in the labour market. In 1948 the British Nationality Act was passed, which conferred the status of British citizenship on all people from countries within the British Commonwealth – the group of countries under British rule – allowing them full rights of entry and settlement.

The first ship that brought a large group of West Indian immigrants to the United Kingdom was the *Empire Windrush*, a former German passenger liner.

It arrived at Tilbury Dock in Essex on 22 June 1948 with 492 passengers (and several stowaways) on board – men and women from Jamaica, Tobago, Trinidad and other Caribbean islands. Many of them were ex-servicemen who had fought for Britain in the War. And many of them had been urged to come by enticing advertisements in newspapers, proclaiming Britain as the 'Mother Country' and promising jobs and a better standard of living.

When these new arrivals walked down the gangplank, taking their first steps towards what they hoped would be a brighter future, they could not have imagined that their journey was the start of a wave of mass migration that would change the social landscape of Britain. The Caribbean people who came to Britain as part of this post-war movement later became known as the 'Windrush Generation'.

The *Windrush* passengers were met by the press on arrival, and later that day the *Evening Standard* greeted them with the headline, 'Welcome Home!' But despite this initially warm welcome, the immigrants found that conditions were not what they might have been expecting. The country was only just beginning to recover from the devastation caused by the War and there was a severe housing shortage. Many of the *Windrush* passengers had to be temporarily housed in the air-raid shelter under Clapham Common. They found the climate and differences in available food an uncomfortable challenge. And, worse, they also faced discrimination and racism. Unofficial 'colour bars' were introduced and signs featuring slogans such as 'No Coloured, Dogs or Irish' were common. They were often treated as second-class citizens with regard to employment, housing, access to education and treatment by the police. There was hostility and sometimes violence, which worsened during the 1950s and lead to race riots in cities, including London and Birmingham.

But despite enduring this prejudice, the Caribbean community embraced Britain in the firm belief that the 'Mother Country' valued and cared for all its subjects. They settled in London (many of them in Brixton, close to where the original *Windrush* passengers were housed) and around the country, established churches and community centres, and actively participated in the few organizations that opened their doors to them such as trade unions and local councils. Many of them found jobs working for essential public services such as the newly formed NHS, British Rail and the Royal Mail. By the 1970s, West Indians had become an integral part of the fabric of British society, influencing and impacting on everything from culture to politics.

The Windrush Generation played a significant role in shaping and creating modern Britain. Their contribution to the workforce helped to make Britain one of the most successful post-war economies in Europe – and, perhaps even more importantly, their arrival and their emphasis on the values of hard work, empathy and respect helped to shape the country into one of the most vibrant and tolerant multicultural societies in the world.

Victoria Walters, Editor

About the Author

Floella Benjamin was born on the Caribbean island of Trinidad in 1949, and came to England in 1960 as part of the Windrush generation. She has enjoyed a successful career as a children's presenter, best known for the iconic BBC TV programmes *Play School* and *Play Away*, and has also worked as an actress, writer, producer, working peer and an active advocate for the welfare and education of children. Her broadcasting work has been recognized with a Special Lifetime Achievement BAFTA and an OBE. She was appointed a Baroness in the House of Lords in 2010 and a Dame in the 2020 New Year Honours list, and is the Chair of the Windrush Commemoration Committee.

About the Illustrator

Joelle Avelino is a Congolese and Angolan London-based illustrator. She graduated from the University of Hertfordshire with a BA (Hons) in Illustration with Marketing degree in 2012. She works with both traditional and digital methods of drawing and painting to create her vibrant and distinctive illustrations. She is greatly inspired by phenomenal women, everyday life and her African heritage particularly. Having grown up in the UK, Joelle aims to bring these two worlds together through her work.

Don't ...

classic memoir, written by Floella Benjamin and
fully illustrated by Diane Ewen for 2-5 year-olds.

Perfect for bringing Floella's inspiring Windrush
story to a new generation of young readers.